Unspoken

Unspoken

A collection of untold intersex stories

Georgia Andrews, Bee, Antoinette Briffa,
Paul Byrne-Moroney, Morgan Carpenter,
Jocelyn Dalton, CJ (Carolyn) Hannaford,
Bonnie Hart, Phoebe Hart, Jelly,
Steph Lum, Mani Bruce Mitchell,
Sandra Perrin, Cody Smith and others

Unspoken acknowledges the traditional owners of the land on which these memories were written and drawn, and on which we live, grow and connect.

Unspoken acknowledges that sovereignty was never ceded.

Always was. Always will be. Aboriginal land.

For intersex people everywhere who continue to find words that fit what they have seen, heard or felt.
Thank you for your strength, courage and beauty.

For parents, know that unconditional love is the best beginning possible.

~

In memory of Jocelyn Dalton

Cover art: Olympia Balopitos

Intersex Peer Support Australia: https://isupport.org.au/
YOUth&I: https://youthandi.org/

Unspoken © 2023 Intersex Peer Support Australia
Copyright remains with the writers and artists

ISBN: 978-0-6456726-0-2

FOREWORD

A CONVERSATION WITH
BONNIE HART, FORMER PRESIDENT OF
INTERSEX PEER SUPPORT AUSTRALIA AND
STEPH LUM, EDITOR OF UNSPOKEN

Steph: Here we are, speaking the unspoken.

Bonnie: Yeah, we've been working on this for a while now! In my undergraduate psychology degree, I came across feminist memory work as a grassroots method to work within groups. It aims to build trust and explore experiences that are not written into other histories and I was like, that would just be *so good* for our intersex support group! We had an upcoming retreat for IPSA [Intersex Peer Support Australia], which was still the AISSGA [Androgen Insensitivity Syndrome Support Group Australia] at the time. I thought it'd be a great activity to do.

Steph: And it was! You gave us all prompts related to moments in our past and you let us decide whether we wrote a page or we drew something or both. We didn't have to participate if we didn't want to but so many of us did. As someone who did, it was such a nice, reflective moment to take some time away from that retreat to sit by myself and put something onto paper. It was really touching because I remember we all came back together and we sat around like a big family and you read through the whole thing. It was really beautiful.

Bonnie: Yeah, I think that flexibility was what made it really work well with the group. Because those support retreats can be really full on—lots of talking, lots of connecting and lots of people going deep into things that they haven't talked about before. So some people who chose not to do the exercise really just took that time to either connect one on one with someone else or to just take time out to sit with themselves.

Steph: This took place in 2017. How did you find the experience of running this activity in Australia, in Kingston outside of Daylesford (Dja Dja Wurrung land) and then also in Auckland, Aotearoa (New Zealand) later that year?

Bonnie: It was really great to do the same activity in both spaces. People in Aotearoa were as equally open to the idea. It was like ducks to water, having this new format to be able to do some deeper reflection. Writing in the third-person created narrative distance from their first-person emotions and allowed people to describe things in great detail looking at the context, as opposed to the impact, of a lot of the situations that they experienced.

Steph: As someone participating, I'd never thought about writing about any of this in the third-person before. As someone who's very, you know, *shy*, I don't like to share much about myself, but making it third-person I felt like I could be a lot more honest. Even though it was still me writing there's that creation of distance somehow.

Because it was anonymous as well, I just felt like for the first time I could actually just write something that was true of this experience, like an observer to that experience, in a way.

Bonnie: It makes a lot of sense. It is about creating a different angle of viewing to see things in a different light. I often talk about my intersex lived experiences as being a kind of invisible history that I have to throw paint at from different directions to get the full scope of it. Just standing from one point and looking, you don't see the true depth. You actually don't know what you don't know until you throw something chaotically from another direction and then all of a sudden, a new aspect or intersection that you may not have thought about before becomes apparent.

Steph: There are so few books out there that share our intersex experiences and even fewer by intersex people. Can you share a bit of the context of this lack of intersex voices in the community and this lack of understanding about what intersex is?

Bonnie: This exercise was run in a three day retreat for people who had any innate variation of sex characteristics. I suppose the capacity to be connected in that kind of way, irrespective of what your body is like or the specific diagnostic terms used to talk about your body, is quite new in Australia. So there's a dual aspect of there being such a little amount of knowledge in society about intersex and then people with variations of sex characteristics often have such limited language to talk about their bodies. People use the language that they've been taught by clinicians, by their parents. Language can be quite a prison, limiting some ways of thinking, but it's also an opportunity for connection. Having access to language means that we're able to say things about ourselves that we wouldn't necessarily have said. It helps create points of connection with other people and increased opportunity for support.

Steph: I think that's one of the most powerful things about these intersex community retreats is just that meeting of people, learning about new experiences and so much knowledge sharing. So many people don't know that other variations exist and there are different ways to talk about yourself or think about yourself or even just live your life. They're so empowering in that sense.

Bonnie: Yeah, heck yeah! So traditionally, lots of support groups have really been diagnostic-specific. Clinicians will often only refer people to support groups related to their diagnosis. The fact that Intersex Peer Support Australia is non-diagnostic specific allows people to connect, not just around the individual manifestation of their particular variation of sex characteristics, but also to connect around their experiences of healthcare, their experiences of social situations or their experiences of disclosure—whether that is having their intersex variation disclosed to them or self-disclosing to other people. These experiences are so common across intersex variations. It's one of the things that makes peer support so important because those threads knit together to create a real social safety net that clinical services can't do alone. They don't have the time to do that, they don't have the flexibility in their frameworks for understanding intersex to accommodate the diversity that is out there in the intersex community.

Steph: You can see, even in just these stories, we do not know what variations the different writers have and yet they could have had almost any intersex variation. These experiences, as you said, at the social level and even physical experiences and treatments, *do* crossover between different variations so closely. All those feelings of isolation and confusion and not knowing what's happening, or those feelings of knowing something is happening but you're not a part of that experience. These seem to crossover through a lot of these stories. Similarly, that feeling of connection when people have found each other and what a change that made for them. They're not talking about finding people with the same diagnosis as they have, they are talking about finding a community of intersex people that supports them and welcomes them for who they are.

Bonnie: These are such powerful records of people's lives across the lifespan. Stories of people when they were young, when they were adults, when they were in relationships, when they were on their own, as they are approaching the end of life. We know that there are very different medical paradigms that people have experienced across the lifespan. I think the youngest participant was 18 and the oldest was 87 in this work.

Steph: Some societal norms have shifted so much in some respects over that period and others, not so much. I would love to see more intersex people writing and drawing and creating, in whatever way they feel comfortable with. Their voices are so valuable and I think so many of us have been told "you're weird", "you're an alien", "you're different" and we don't value our own stories because we don't see them as being important. We're ashamed of it. We want to be on the sidelines because we've had to try to hide our whole lives. I would love it if there was more sharing of our experiences and valuing of it! I think this book is such an important part of that because these stories are incredible. You know, the things that have been shared are so generous and insightful. We have so much to learn. I want people who are intersex to see that in themselves as well.

FOREWORD

Bonnie: I completely agree. Putting these words together allows other people to learn and makes the path so much easier for future generations. The more that's known, the easier it is—the greater the lexicon, the more resources that people have, the richer the discourse, the better words we have to talk about each other, our bodies, our experiences, and what we want. Often it's really hard to dream, because we don't know the landscape of what is possible. So, putting that in words and wrapping it in creativity, kindness and life really is about taking intersex bodies out of clinical spaces and giving people the keys back to their futures.

Steph: Yes—intersex story-telling as life-giving, future-creating! What a privilege to be a part of this collection of intersex stories.

FOREWORD

1

It was always a day filled with mixed emotions she couldn't quite name. For a start, going to see the specialist required a day off from school and a trip into the city with her mum. It made her feel special to dress in nice clothes, on a day where her brothers and friends were at school. Her mum would drive part of the way and then they would catch the tram in for the rest. It was a novelty and there would usually be a minty or some tic-tacs in mum's handbag for the trip. Then there was the waiting room, with toys she felt a little too old to play with and magazines she was too young to be interested in.

When she was called into the office to see the doctor, the day would change. Sometimes it seemed like a quick visit, where he would talk to her mum and then have a look at her tummy—she would startle when he touched her, as she was ticklish. He was one of the few people who would ever get to see her 'bag'. For some reason she was OK with this. For her, her tummy with its criss-cross landscape of scars and the bag were kind of neutral. The area that wasn't neutral lay below her underpants and this was the area she dreaded being seen by anyone. On the occasions where he would not look beneath her underpants she would leave his office feeling fine. She would look forward to the bakery treat she knew she would share with her mum on the return trip.

But there were other times, where he would abruptly pull at the elastic and not only peer at her most private parts, but touch the scarred area with his hands and comment about 'what could be done' in the future, to make her more 'normal'. She would feel her face burn with shame and the tears would well. She would leave his office feeling awful and somehow violated. She didn't have the words to describe to her mother how this felt. Instead, she wouldn't mention it, in the hope that this would minimise or erase what had just happened. On these occasions, any bakery treat would stick like a lump in her throat. The smug feeling of having a day off school would evaporate and another layer of shame and secrecy would be draped around her shoulders.

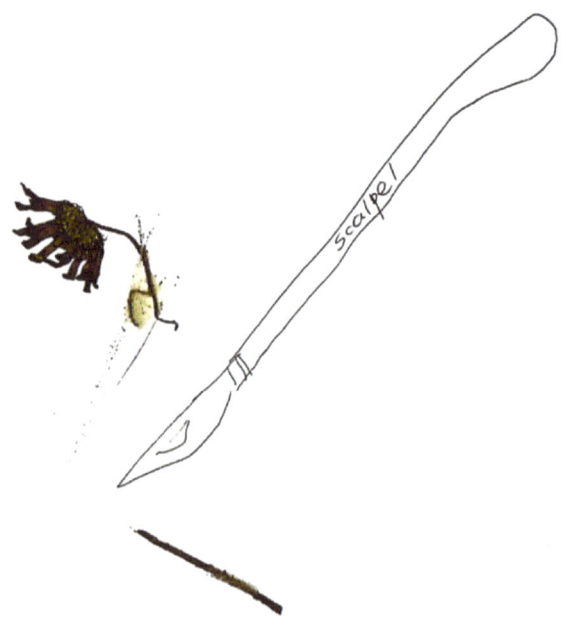

II

Her body was first examined by her GP at the age of 16 or 17. She can't exactly remember. She had been experiencing cyclical abdominal pains and had not had a period—so her mother dragged her to the doc where, upon examination, her GP discovered what she assumed was a thick hymen.

"Easy to fix!"

A simple day surgery was planned, secrecy and trust assured. The specialist gyno was selected for the task. Friendly and personable, she made her feel like the thick hymen was no big deal. "It's totally normal," they said. "Common, even. Just a small incision."

A 45-minute surgery was booked, instead of what should, retrospectively, have been an ultra-sound investigation. What happened in this surgery has only been recently discovered, 10 years later—the 'small incision' revealed no vaginal canal, so cutting was continued deep into the tissue mass until a small opening was discovered. At this point, an inflation device was inserted and inflated, stretching the area. Cutting continued as this was not so successful. At some point, the surgeon realised there was no vagina and she was actually dilating the patient's urethra. Perhaps this happened when the patient started leaking urine. The 45-minute surgery turned into a 4-hour operation with a urologist called in to 'repair' the problem.

She woke up in recovery, a concerned mother waiting. The gyno walked into the shared ward and loudly exclaimed, "We couldn't find your vagina." She did not tell the patient why she had woken up in a lot of pain and why she had a catheter. The patient felt confused and scared. She was unsure what this meant. When the gyno announced that she would 'fix this', the patient was relieved. As was her mother.

When she finally returned home, she did not discuss this with her siblings or parents again, or her friends at school. She was in pain and subsequently incontinent. She leaked urine constantly and had to bring a change of clothing to school each day. She decided it was best not to think about it much, as the gyno was on the case to sort it all out. After weeks passed and no improvement (as promised) was felt with the incontinence, her mother tried to track the specialist down, only to discover that she had left the hospital.

She was not informed as to why she did not have a vagina and whether this was part of any sort of physiological characteristic. She was told however that she was 'very rare' but her disorder could be fixed so she would be like a normal woman.

"No one would ever have to know."

She felt that all the focus was on the physical and no mention was ever made of how this might psychologically impact her. So, this is how she approached the problem. She looked forward to being fixed and putting this all behind her. It was better to not think about it.

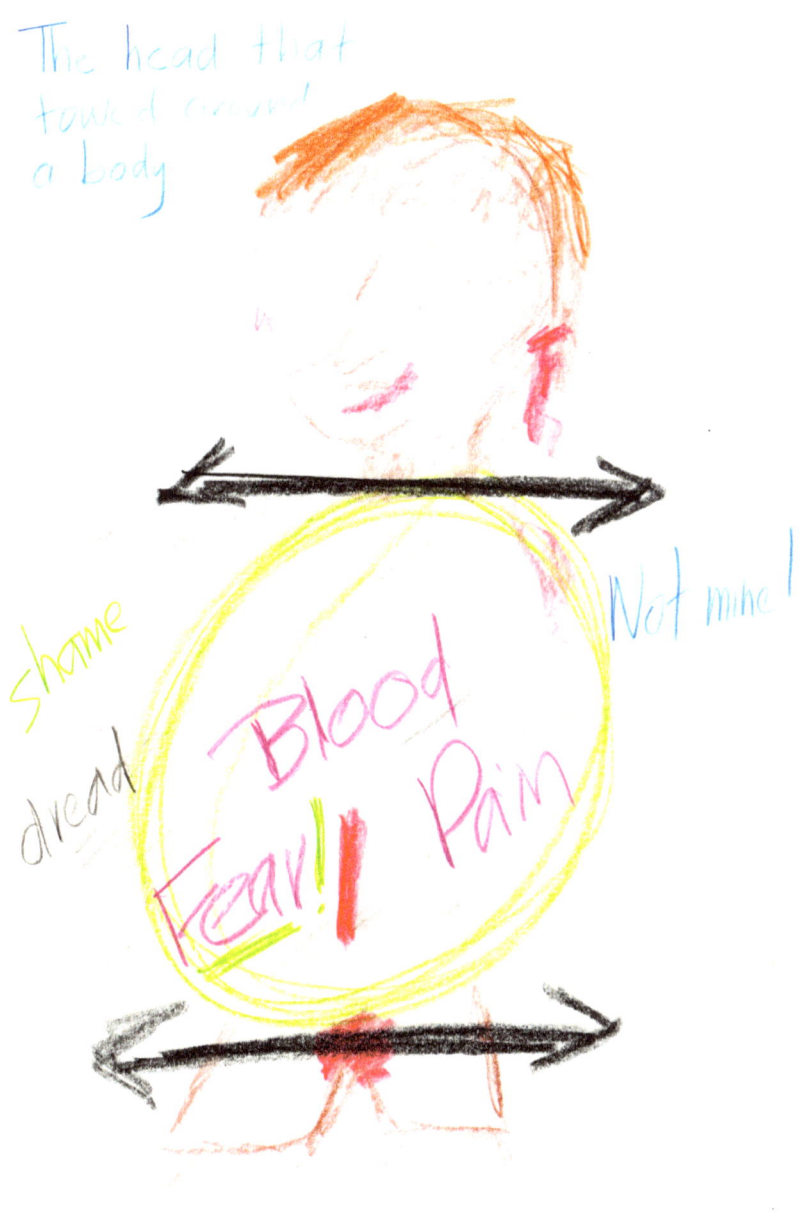

III

The phone rings. The girl is walking to the beach with her boarding school sisters on a Sunday afternoon. She is contemplating whether to play volleyball next to the sand dunes, sunbathe on the grass, or hit the water in an attempt to draw the eye of a cute guy at the skatepark.

Irritatingly, the phone continues to blast an obnoxious Nokia ringtone. She contemplates ignoring the call—it's probably her mother, ringing for the 100th time today to see if she's settled into her new classes. In a Mary Poppin's-like fashion, she deposits half of her worldly possessions onto the ground and extracts her phone from the depths of the unknown.

Screen flashing...heart racing...the doctor's name appears on Caller ID. Embedded into the screen.

She suddenly realises that they must have her test results. Last week they thought she had brain cancer but the tests were all totally clear. Today is Sunday and it's a holiday weekend—what the hell is going on?!

The doctor is very quiet. She apologises for calling on the weekend and asks the girl how she is. She asks if she has a quiet place to talk. The girl lets her 120 housemates abandon her down the road as she stands on a mossy embankment, under a tree.

Bluntly, the doctor said that she has been sent 'conclusive results', results that had been previously misread by another doctor as being negative. The results required urgent consultation with a specialist by the end of the week. The doctor continued to tell the girl she had only ever considered these results as being a 'worst case scenario', her parents had already been informed, and she would have to take a day or two off school, meet with her parents, then a new doctor would explain everything.

In less than 5 minutes the conversation was over.

The girl had been told she was abnormal. She was told this was urgent, requiring specialist care, a WORST CASE scenario.

She heard all of this. Under a tree. Standing in the moss.

Alone.

IV

Laid out on the slab. Under a sheet. It had all built up to this. All the trips to the doctors, all the examinations of her genitals. All the cold fingers.

It was finally show time.

She felt a bit scared, alone in that room, when the doctor finally came in talking to about eight other people she had never seen before. The doc said, "We're just going to take a little look." Again! she thought. Then he said to his friends, "See how…and she doesn't have…and she won't…" Everyone leaned in to see what was between her splayed legs.

"And see if I do this…" and he put his cold fingers inside her tiny vagina. She jumped at the sensation and he said, "A bit cold hey?" before turning back to his friends and saying the blind vagina only has a limited depth whilst pushing deeper into her vaginal pouch. He pushed so hard that she farted and giggled. That made him remove his hands from her and wash them with some antiseptic wash.

She was 12 and realised her body was not her own.

UNSPOKEN

V

Whenever he'd had a general anaesthetic, that he could remember, he would be asked multiple times by nurses and doctors during the preparation process for surgery what procedure was being done. He thought it was so they can make sure that the correct procedure was being done. Something about avoiding negligence, maybe? Consent? Anyway, there's only one time this didn't happen: when he had a gonadectomy. No questions asked. No reminders during the surgical preparation about what was going to happen. It's like it was unmentionable, or even the worst kind of thing that could happen. If they can't even say it, how could he even begin to think about it, and talk about it?

VI

She was 16 years old and still hadn't menstruated. After her parents made several GP appointments, all asking her, "Have you had your period yet?" she knew something was up. Reluctantly, she agreed to go to see a specialist, "Just to see how much taller you are going to grow", said her Mum. But when she got to the doctor, out came that question again, "Have you had your period yet?" No! She was getting fed up with doctors asking her the same thing. This time though, he wanted to check her vagina, "Just to make sure everything's OK." She reluctantly agreed, and afterwards left the doctor's surgery in tears. She felt scared and alone. "What is wrong with me?" At the time this was all going on, she was a very, very busy girl. She liked being busy because it stopped her thinking about things too much. She was doing ballet, studying Year 11 at night school, and fitting in one or two casual jobs. She didn't have time for all these medical appointments and stupid doctors asking embarrassing questions. She didn't want to know about it, so she pretended everything was fine and just kept a smiling face that hid the turmoil she felt underneath.

But then came the day she knew that her body was different, really different. Her parents got the news first, from a bigwig gynaecologist at a university, a professor no less. "I must have a really serious problem if a professor has to work it out," she thought. That night, her father picked her up as usual from the tech college, and she jumped in the driver's seat so she could get driving practice for her P plates.

"So how did the doctor's appointment go?" she asked her Dad.

He looked a bit serious and said they would talk about it when they got home.

"But I want to know now."

She couldn't wait that long, she wanted to know what the hell was going on. And so he told her, "Your ovaries aren't working properly, you don't have a uterus, and the doctor says it's best to get your ovaries removed."

Her whole world caved in at that moment. Time stopped and she was in shock. Her Dad asked if she was OK to drive.

"Yes, I'm fine," she said. She was good at pretending, really good.

So that was when everything changed, and her journey towards discovering she had Androgen Insensitivity Syndrome began. It wasn't until 10 years later she learnt the whole truth, that her 'ovaries' were actually testes, and that she would discover a whole community of amazing people like her.

VII

She never wanted to develop into a woman anyway. She thought she had been unlucky to be born female and when puberty started, she accepted with resignation that her body would inevitably change into something she didn't want it to be. She didn't understand there could be another way of being.

Puberty started—but then it never really went anywhere.

11, 12. Some girls already had their periods.
13, 14. Other bodies were noticeably different now.
15, 16. Some girls could pass as much older than they were, but she still looked like a young child.
17, 18. Everyone assumed she had her period by now. Maybe she still looked young and was a slow developer, but surely by now…

She didn't really mind, though. It's not like she wanted to get her period anyway. She felt like she was waiting. Waiting. Waiting for something she didn't really want but which she knew must come. Waiting—to understand? Because while she didn't mind her body was different, she didn't understand the world that everyone around her lived in. Of periods, boys, drama, sex. She thought she didn't understand because she hadn't fully developed, and once she had then it would all make sense and maybe she would be part of that world. Her parents assumed she had her period already—they knew she was fiercely independent and not a big sharer. It made her laugh to think they didn't really believe her when she told them otherwise.

Why all the discussion of periods? She was raised to believe that that was the defining moment into womanhood. Until then, she was still a child, and a child who just didn't really understand what everyone else was on about.

Then she found out that her milestone into womanhood would never come. That she had probably gone through puberty years ago. That maybe all those things that she didn't understand—well, maybe she would never understand. At least now she didn't have to keep waiting.

VIII

Revenge fantasy

She stood over the quivering man, lying bloodied and moaning, with the mashed stump of his cock gagging him from making any other sound.

My doctor. Herr Doktor.

Now he was hers to play with as she pleased and the crimson tide flowing from his mutilated groin was evidence of her capricious, murderous will. She toyed with the blood-smeared scalpel and smiled. A million possibilities ran through her mind like a smorgasbord of sadistic delights.

"Should I assail him with my silver blade once more, scarring his body with my hand? Should I pin him like a specimen, splayed wide for my inspecting probes to violate?"

No. Those visceral options were short-term. They offered no lasting access to the pleasure she so wantonly craved. Finally, it occurred to her. Ruin his corporeal form by inflicting wounds that would—in time—be survived; unless, of course, she decided to end his pathetic life here and now. But no! She deserved meat for a while longer. The recourse she settled on was far more seductive and subtle. She would convince him *he* was the one to blame for the grievous wounds she had inflicted upon him! He would thank me for taking my surgical weapon to his body the way he'd so callously taken it to mine years earlier. She could not help but grin as she slipped her hand into her undies and straddled his writhing body...

It was time for her to get her freak on!

UNSPOKEN

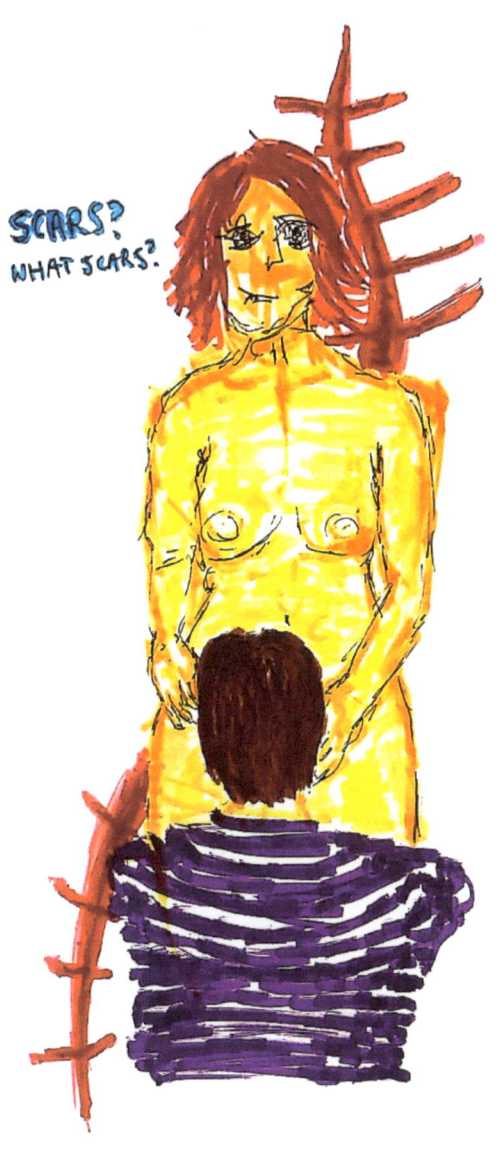

IX

She discovered she was unable to have children when she was five by overhearing her parents talking. That always made her feel less of a girl growing up. The most difficult situations she'd had discussing her inability to have children had been with male partners. Having children was important to her and being infertile (and not a 'normal' woman) was a huge issue. It made her feel less valued as a woman and considerably less valued as a woman in a relationship with a man.

She told her ex-husband very early on in their relationship and he was great. They ended up fostering children. That really helped overcome her issues with being infertile although she did regret never having had periods, being pregnant, giving birth, and raising a child from infancy. Now that she was older—and in a lesbian relationship—being infertile was less of an issue. Her wife had a hysterectomy a few years ago, so it now felt like her partner was in the same situation as her.

X

For her whole adult life, up until this point, she thought she was the only person in the whole world to have this 'awful' thing called 'testicular feminisation'—and certainly couldn't imagine shouting that phrase from the rooftops and seeing if anyone else out there might answer. Nobody had ever suggested she talk to someone about it (e.g. a counsellor who might have been able to shed some light on the subject). It was the 1970s and 1980s, pre-internet, and where would you find information that might suggest there were others of your 'species' out there? Besides which, she had been patted on the head by the surgeon after her 'corrective' surgery at 16 and told to just 'get on with it'. She met her future husband 8 months later and settled into trying to have that promised 'perfect life', so the need to tell or find others faded against other life priorities—work, building a house, getting on the adoption list etc.

But the marriage became troubled due to domestic violence, and she sought help for THAT. She went to see a counsellor and her 'condition' was touched on briefly, but her focus was on saving her marriage, not herself.

A divorce followed and at age 30 she found herself starting life all over again. It was like being 16 years old again. Occasionally, the curiosity about herself would come to the fore, especially when she reached the point in her new life where she contemplated having a physical, sexual relationship. The turning point was an extended visit to the USA in 1995—she was 43 years old. She had time on her hands (which was not usual). She was a bit bored in Grants Pass, Oregon where she was staying with a friend, and finished up in the local library. It was here she stumbled upon some medical information talking about AIS (Androgen Insensitivity Syndrome—the 'new' name for her condition) and mention of a USA support group, which on further checking referred to an Australian Support Group—the AISSGA.

Once back home in Australia she eventually made contact with the group, and was invited to attend the annual conference in Melbourne. With both excitement and trepidation, she ventured there and met, for the first time, members of what she now calls her 'other' family.

In what you might think was a 'safe' place for discovery and sharing, she still found it quite confronting—because indeed she was confronting her real self for probably the first time, as much as she was meeting others of her ilk. It was revelatory. Hearing other people's stories and telling her own, she was filled with tears. She felt 'normal' with these people. But it was just the beginning of a very long journey of self-discovery lasting over the next 20 years, and one that possibly won't ever end.

She knew she was part of the intersex community, as common as people with red hair (about 1.7–2%), and, in her words, was no longer 'the freak show of the circus'. She was so thankful to every one of those intersex friends she met at that first conference and every one since.

UNSPOKEN

XI

They met at a 'hippie festival' following a workshop. He was spiritual, handsome and confident—or so she thought. In actual fact, unbeknownst to her, his outward confidence hid a secret; a morbid shyness and fear that, until recently, he had kept hidden for more than 20 years. He was actually extremely body conscious and just 6 months before had been diagnosed with an intersex variation. While she couldn't wait to get him into bed, intimacy was his greatest fear. Exposing his abnormal genitalia, regardless of his excruciating lust for women, was an idea he couldn't imagine and couldn't bear.

After returning from the festival, they went their separate ways but having similar interests and some cross-over with their friends' networks, they met again some weeks later. They spoke at a party, reminisced about the festival, and then she gave him a lift home.

That night changed his life. When they arrived home, they sat together in the car and continued to talk. Then, without notice, she leaned over and kissed him. It felt amazing and they became quite passionate. He was feeling her and she began to touch him. First his upper body and then, naturally, began to massage his groin. At first, he was taken aback but he said nothing and before long decided his inhibitions had held him back long enough. He decided to go with the flow.

And flow it did. After two more dates they decided to date formally, and then it happened. He invited her to come in, they stripped off slowly and she never said a word. She didn't even seem to notice he had balls the size of sparrow's eggs. They both just enjoyed the moment and by the end of the evening they had fulfilled each other completely. It was exhilarating, freeing and completely natural.

It turned out he had nothing to fear and it turned out she had been just as nervous as him. They both experienced a paradigm shift and fell in love.

XII

They never told a lie about their body, not knowingly. How was it possible to tell the truth about your body without knowing what intersex was? What language is used to describe it? There were no secrets between them and their friends.

"How did you get that scar?" she asked.
"Surgery. The doctors had to do something to fix it," they answered. Not a lie.

The scar lined up with where they understood their kidneys to be. It made sense and there was no way to know better. Not a lie.

"You weren't at school yesterday?" another friend asks.
"I had to go see a doctor in Sydney," they answer.
"Why Sydney?"
"I'm not sure."
"Are you sick?"
"I don't think so. They just took an x-ray and some blood tests."

Couldn't know better. Not a lie.

"Ugh, with a needle?" She wrinkles her nose.
"Yes, it was pretty gross. I read the new animorphs though."

Later in life, change rooms became an issue.

"Always early, first to get dressed," the PE teacher marvelled. It's because they feel alien in their skin, but they don't have the words to say why.

"I figure if I always help set up, you won't notice I'm terrible at sport," they joke. Not a lie, also true. The joke deflects but it also justifies. It tries to understand.

"But really, why are you always first to PE?" their best friend asks later. When a joke is known to be shifting the truth.

"I don't want people figuring out I like girls," they answer. Not a joke this time, but still deflecting from a truth impossible to acknowledge. It's a blurry line now. Were they lying to their teacher? Their best friend? Themselves? Or was it simply the best possible explanation in the absence of truth?

Finding out they were intersex wasn't so much the last piece of a puzzle, but more like finding the first piece of a new puzzle. New things to understand, to learn, to live their truth at last. But starting again, trying to re-learn how the pieces fit together. It was hard; they were fraying. When asked if they were okay, old conversations became new again.

"I found out I'm intersex," they answer.
"What does that mean?" she asks.
"Sometimes babies are born with things that make them different from how boys and girls are born. At least, that's how I understand it," they answer.

"That's why you have those scars," she points out.

"Yeah. And why I had to see the doctor in Sydney." Not lies; new truths.

"Of course! I almost forgot about that. Wow, that's wild. Are you okay?" their best friends asks.

"Yeah," they lie.

XIII

They went into the room—a comfortable 1980s house. Remarkable but for one aspect. It faced out over a harbour framed by two giant pohutukawa trees, red in their Christmas splendour.

Nervous, they asked the question: "What happened when I was born?"

Mother, a white middle-aged woman, answered in a somewhat remote, rural pragmatic voice. "Oh, we were in Auckland staying with Meg and Bob and my waters broke early in the morning. Dad got up, got the car ready (the era when cars had to be started and warmed up before they could move). We drove into Auckland—fast wishing a traffic cop would come—but none did. Arrived at the Maternity hospital around 6.30—the matron met us."

Mother models the stern matron's arms folded. "I am sorry Mrs Laird you can't have your baby yet there are no doctors available..." She directs the mother to go and wait in the birthing room with the young nurse.

Remote, the mother returns from her memory fog.

"You were born about 20 minutes later. The nurse bent down, picked you up and said 'Oh my god, it's a hermaphrodite!'."

The mother, this woman connected with this deep visceral trauma memory, started screaming and ran out of the room.

They are left standing, shocked, confused by what has just happened. Never have they seen their mother express emotion, certainly nothing like that.
What was the screaming about?
What was this word 'hermaphrodite'?
How did it locate to the skin of the person in the room?

Ten minutes later the mother returned—eyes red from crying. She, the mother, looked out of the window—it's a sunny blue sky day. She turns and said, "You know what dear, I think it's going to rain—we better go and get the washing in."

The two people descended the back steps and walked to the washing line. Both knew a dreadful secret has been accidentally liberated from its putrid stink box. Nothing is said… but in the silence of the clacking clothes pegs both agreed to never speak about this again.

In the front of the house, waves gently break on the shore. A pohutukawa flower breaks free, its redness flutters silently to the ground. It knows the words will come again, it knows the mother will take her crippling pain to her death. They will find a place to tell the story but that will not happen for another 30 years.

XIV

The most shameless thing she had done to flaunt her intersexy would definitely be appearing in her own single intersexy float—one year after coming out as intersex.

She felt so proud, free and liberated to wave the intersex flag at Mardi Gras. It had taken courage, strength and inner conviction to do this. It was an amazing event! She was so proud to wave the intersex flag, to present an intersex presence. She was accompanied by OUTLine, a phone counselling service, and her partner who was very supportive. The crowds were very encouraging. There was a great sense of community—the rainbow community.

The day after the event she felt satisfied that she had made the right decision to take part in Mardi Gras even though she was the only intersex participant. She felt a sense of accomplishment. It confirmed to her that she had made the right decision to come out as intersex to her partner, family and friends, and to the wider world at large. It felt great to claim her intersex identity.

XV

Growing up, their life was shrouded in secrets and guises. One face for this group and one for another. Secrets kept behind closed doors. Don't tell anyone for fear you will be outed and judged. Their life was a minefield. Tip-toeing. Treading lightly. Not being seen or noticed.

Don't tell...secrets...live a life of secrets...NO!!!

The hardest part of life is being in it. Everyone has their secrets. Everyone has their fear.

Break the cycle...give voice...

They couldn't pinpoint the moment in time, but the knowledge that their life was full of people that loved them for the person they were gave them the power to ignore the negativity. Given the power to live a life outside of the norm. To be a part of the chosen few with strengths and knowledge others could only imagine. Living a life without expectation or program. Living a life of freedom, awareness and sensitivity. Embracing the differences and variances of all beings and letting those in oneself be embraced.

XVI

She never understood why she rarely felt the need to satisfy herself. When her friends would come back from a night out and share their sexual exploits, she felt mystified that she hardly had the urge to take someone by the hand and lead them to the bedroom. Sure, she was timid to share her body and her secrets with someone. But more than that, she lacked the drive that would otherwise free up her courage. Until well into her thirties, in fact, sexual intimacy would become satisfying but not necessary fulfilling. Her "Os" were quick and fleeting, if they happened at all.

And then, like a white knight on a black stallion, her saviour rode into her life: Mr T. He was more than any mortal man could give her: he was *The Urge*. This Mr T, this shot in the ass of testosterone, opened up doors she had never known before with just a few injections. The desire began to course through her body. As she learned to work with the feeling—the embrace and savour it—she also opened up to the warmth of her own touch. And, my... it was fulfilling—it was The O.

Eventually, she would also learn to share that with a trusted other. Her fairy tale of sexual fulfilment had finally come true.

XVII

He sat alone on a singular window seat of the school bus on the way home that day, which was a little unusual for him. He was a well-liked young lad and would usually be down the back with his friends getting involved in whatever mischievous activity had taken their favour to fill the half hour bus journey.

But today was different.

He wanted solitude, wanted to stare out the bus window and brood on something that was troubling him. Most of the other kids were full of excitement on this particular day, as it was the last day of school for the first semester. Most kids were boasting about the adventures they had planned or arranging sleepovers with friends over the two-week holiday period. He knew this was customary behaviour in which he would usually partake in, however he knew these holidays were going to be different for him and not so pleasurable.

The previous weeks leading up to the holidays had been quite stressful—doctor's appointments and long explanatory discussions with his mother confirmed that he would spend the first few days of the school holidays in hospital undergoing another dreaded surgery. He had almost become accustomed to them by now, however this time he couldn't help but feel deceived by his mother. She had said the previous surgery was to be the last and now another one.

He was almost 9 now and wondered how much longer he could continue to hide his secret from his school friends.

He was snatched from his deep thinking when he felt something land on the back of his shirt collar. He reached around and grabbed the wet gooey object. He smiled and instantly recognised what it was—a spit ball. He turned to the rear of the bus to see his friend, Nathan, with a big guilty grin and proceeded to give him the finger. As he turned back towards the front of the bus, he noticed his older brother and his friend look back at him from the front of the bus with a look of guilt and suspicious intensity on their faces.

He and his brother were close in age and had become very competitive in recent years, constantly fighting over things and going to extreme measures to prove superiority over one another. He was now watching his brother talking to his friend, and started to have his own suspicious thoughts about what they were discussing. Reading other people's expressions and behaviours was an instinct he had unknowingly developed from an early age to help deal with his circumstance.

He realised his stop was rapidly approaching and, grabbing his school bag, started making his way towards the exit door. His friend called out, "See you at my sleep over," in which he replied with a lie "Yeah, see you then," and kept walking to avoid further discussion.

Now, waiting at the exit as the bus came to a complete stop, the automated doors opened and his brother shoved past him, exiting the bus like it was some kind of race. He shook his head and called out, "Wanker!" As he stepped off the bus, his brother's friend asked, "Hey, is it true you are having an operation on your dick?"

He stepped off the bus and the automated doors closed.

XVIII

She felt very self-conscious about herself when she was a teenager because she felt other people would detect that she had something wrong with her, and she was ashamed of herself.

Other girls did not have her condition, so the best way forward was to *pretend* she was okay. This involved living somewhat in the shadows, involving herself in physical exercise where she would feel *strong* and able to face up to life. She tried some medication later in life: alcohol helped, but neither of these so-called aids suited her sense of integrity—that was a sham way to live—so she resisted.

Another little 'ritual' that helped was to spend time in the sun whenever possible. The sunshine gave her confidence—all of this was due to her fears of being exposed to the world as a girl who was a disappointment to her family.

Such rituals can last a lifetime but growing older has helped.

XIX

She was a young woman, having left the family culture, out there in the world. Living in share accommodation, at university, with a part time job. She was still mortally afraid of intimacy and relationships, having not had sex since a disastrous attempt when she was 14. A boy she was keen on, who felt safe, was going to this rainbow gathering in the country. She decided she would go and see what happened.

She finished work late and drove for several hours in the middle of the night. She went a strange way and at some point passed a sign to the town she was heading to, pointing down a windy dirt road. Thinking it was a short cut, she took the road. This path led deep into the forest. She had already been driving for hours but wasn't confident to turn around. Feeling she was lost, she asked for a sign if she was heading the right way. At that moment a white owl flew into the windscreen of her car. She shat herself! She was so afraid, alone in the woods, lost, that she couldn't stop. She didn't check to see if the owl was hurt…or real. She also didn't turn back but put her foot down and screamed away into the wrong direction. The trip to the gathering that should have been 3 hours took her 8. She was exhausted when she arrived and crashed out in the welcoming tent.

The next day when she woke she headed down to the gathering to find her friend. Although she was quite involved with alternative culture, she found hippy styles a bit threatening with all the casual flesh people displayed. Now she was in a zone where people were 'free' and cruising round the camp completely naked. She was wearing pretty hippy clothes except for these old Nike sneakers she'd been given from someone who was throwing them out. She felt so judged to be wearing these sweatshop manufactured corporate symbols of oppression on her oversized feet. She found her friends' camp but they weren't there.

Someone told her they were down the river having a swim. Now, she LOVED swimming—the water, the freedom and buoyancy. She also felt pretty skanky after her horror drive the night before, so she rushed down to the water. There, the river was completely filled with naked hippies. Flesh and hair soup.

She could see her friends in the mix. They saw her and called out and everyone looked…at her inappropriate footwear…judgemental hippies…and she froze on the banks of the river.

She was so insecure. She had never told another person about how her body was different—'underdeveloped'. She just wanted to dive into the water fully clothed but didn't. Everyone was looking at her, waiting for her to strip off her city clothes and join the heteronormative hippy hive.

She turned and ran. Shamed and naked, but still fully clothed.

XX

She heard the kettle boil and knew it was time to enter the kitchen. Time to catch up with the supervisor. Time for small talk about the weather…Trump's latest Twitter rampage…what to have for lunch. As per usual, the conversation would drag on to what had been finished on the to do list….expectations for the day…what she hadn't achieved that week when she went home from the office feeling 'sick'.

Time for an interrogation yet again from the supervisor about her commitment to the role, her lack of focus, limited communication. Time where her emotional wellbeing was questioned. Why was she fearful? Why was she not willing to participate in social events? Why did she act as though she wanted to detach from the current moment? Where was her drive in this role? More questions, hard questions. Why did she need to associate with an online community of intersex people who saw themselves as different? Why was she committing so much of her work time to travelling half way around the globe to visit them? Why could she not just be grounded in where she was today and the privileged situation she sat in. Was she willing to let a community of strangers take over her life? She entered the kitchen, cloaked in a blanket of insecurity.

Waiting next to the kettle was a newspaper article titled 'I am intersex'. Hanne Gaby's photo across a two-page spread...in the local newspaper. Was this really happening?

The kitchen door opened to the open arms of the supervisor. Tears flowed. A hug that lasted for what seemed like a lifetime. An understanding after four years of why she had seemed distanced. The supervisor could finally start to understand the complex nature of the situation, as portrayed through Hanne's story. The isolation. The confusion. The manipulation. The lies. The way shame draws an individual to withdraw...to question their identity...their purpose.

The article drew words to form a dialogue from what previously could not be spoken and was conceived as a nightmare. The article drew clear that this intersex story was relevant, *important*, one to be heard. The article drew acceptance, shaped a way forward for conversation and spoke a story that in so many ways reflected hers. She was able to finally feel safe to take off her coat, to be openly vulnerable, to be her true self, to ask for support.

This was just the beginning.

XXI

Her last endocrinologist appointment presented her with challenges and some disappointments. She was pleased to visit a new endocrinologist—a new face and a different perspective to the treatment of intersex. Her previous endo she had seen since she was 19 and a half, from the first time they discovered she was intersex. She had a long 35-year history with this endocrinologist. He was like a close family doctor. Someone she looked up to. Someone she trusted and did not doubt his word and advice. For many years, she had wanted to challenge and ask questions about her medical treatment and in particular to ascertain if there was anyone else out there like her—one-in-a-million occurrence with 'testicular insensitivity syndrome'. She had always felt lonely on this intersex journey, shameful, hurt and very frightened of disclosure, so she was always a very private and secretive individual.

Two years after her previous endo retired and she had the opportunity to ask her new endo the questions she had always longed to ask. She was shocked on meeting him when he asked if she had had her 'gonads' removed. Her previous endo and no other medical professional had ever come out with language like this! It was challenging but encouraging because she felt here was someone she could ask pertinent questions. Having only just come 'out' and been in touch with another CAIS (complete androgen insensitivity syndrome) woman she was keen to find out the truth. What was the incidence of her condition? He advised it was more like 1:100,000. She was heartened to hear this. It was better than being told 1:1 million! She asked if he knew of any other person with her intersex condition. He stated he did not. She then summoned the courage to ask, if her condition was not so rare, why wasn't she given the chance, the opportunity to be put in touch with other intersex people (intersex being a term she had only just learnt). He said that it was thought to be of a private nature and that he was not her endo. She said she was fairly happy with the treatment she had received. She felt her previous endo genuinely cared for her—but the thing she struggled with most was the isolation and not having someone to talk to. She said having just met other intersex people, she felt peer support was crucial.

She left the appointment feeling good that she had finally asked these questions but she felt there were 101 questions left unanswered. She also felt his restrained reserve and reticence in answering. Perhaps he had some doubts about her medical care but was not willing to buck the status quo or the endo fraternity in answering them? There are so many questions about her care, the comments made over the years, that were still as yet unanswered!

XXII

As I'm ageing I often—well, not often—I always realise how precious time is.

Each day seems to go faster and time very rarely stands still. I felt my body was always a shameful place and yet when I was young, I allowed my body to be used sexually in a manner that today would be lewd and sickening. Just to get acceptance of some kind and to prove that people like me could have some kind of sex.

Today my body is actually a shrine and nothing about it makes me laugh. I am proud to be who I am, even though certainly not ideally proud of my body. In the past, I would have sex, if that's what you called it, and then many times would vomit afterwards. Today I'm happy for a significant other to hold me, touch me and be with me and my body.

Life and time—the hours, minutes and seconds—are a precious, non-renewable commodity. Coming to terms with what we have, no matter how deformed or different from what some would say the norm is when it comes to our bodies, is a big part of our own healing process and journey to happiness. If we can in some small way come to terms with our bodies, I believe that can help our ability to help others, to continue to seek change for all and all to come.

Age needs to be embraced and savoured; I just wish the rest of the world could embrace and savour any person with a difference, live life, love life and love yourself.

UNSPOKEN

COLLECTIVE STORY INSTRUCTIONS

This is a reflective exercise where you can write a short narrative or draw a picture related to a memory from your lived experience of having intersex traits/innate variations of sex characteristics.

Your work will be compiled alongside others to form a collective story of our experiences. This story may be published in the future as a book and you can select whether or not you would like your work to feature in this, and if so you can opt to be listed as a co-author under your real name, a nom de plume, or anonymously. You can respond to one or all of the questions below - you choose which. You can type in the form or write/draw by hand and upload an image of your work. Would you respond differently in writing than you would typing?

This reflective exercise is designed to bring up memories and feelings that may be painful so that we might look at them with the power and safety of hindsight. If connecting with these memories brings up strong feelings for you that you need help with, reach out

COLLECTIVE STORY INSTRUCTIONS

to your community members for support. You can always contact the folks at Intersex Peer Support Australia at info@isupport.org.au or connect with InterLink at www.ilink.net.au. Our collective story reminds all of us that we are not alone with individual events that happened in our lives.

To start, use the QR code above or head to the online form at isupport.org.au/collective-story.

Writing instructions:

- Write 1 to 2 pages (100-600 words) responding to the memory trigger.
- Write in the third person (she/he/they/...). The advantage of writing in the third person is that we can create personal distance and view the memory from a distance. This helps us avoid justification of the experience.
- Write in as much detail as possible including even what might be considered trivial or inconsequential.
- Describe the experience, don't interpret or explain - leave that to the reader. ;)

Drawing instructions:

- Draw one picture responding to the memory trigger.
- Use whatever medium or style you wish.
- Take a photo of the picture and upload on the last page of the form.

www.ingramcontent.com/pod-product-compliance
Lightning Source LLC
Chambersburg PA
CBHW040838020526
44107CB00071B/1627